# CONTENT

### CHOICE

Fiona Benson • *Midden Witch* • Cape Poetry

### RECOMMENDATIONS

Isabelle Baafi • *Chaotic Good* • Faber & Faber
Ed. Rachael Boast • *Versus Versus: 100 Poems by Deaf, Disabled and Neurodivergent Poets* • Bloodaxe Books
Moya Cannon • *Bunting's Honey* • Carcanet Press
Pascale Petit • *Beast* • Bloodaxe Books

### SPECIAL COMMENDATION

Catherine-Esther Cowie • *Heirloom* • Carcanet Press

### TRANSLATION CHOICE

Jessica Taggart Rose • *The River Has No Colour* •
Translated into French by Claire Durand-Gasselin
The New Menard Press • Bilingual edition

### PAMPHLET CHOICE

Rushika Wick • *Infections of Loss* • Broken Sleep Books

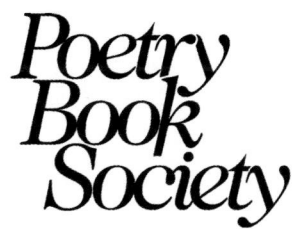

# Poetry Book Society

| | |
|---|---|
| CHOICE SELECTORS RECOMMENDATION SPECIAL COMMENDATION | YOMI ṢODE & VICTORIA KENNEFICK |
| TRANSLATION SELECTOR | SHIVANEE RAMLOCHAN |
| PAMPHLET SELECTORS | YOUSIF M. QASMIYEH & ALYCIA PIRMOHAMED |
| CONTRIBUTORS | SOPHIE O'NEILL MEGAN ROBSON LEDBURY CRITICS THE WRITING SQUAD ROSE SCHIERIG |
| EDITORIAL & DESIGN | ALICE KATE MULLEN |

**Poetry Book Society Memberships**
**Choice**
**4 Books a Year:** 4 Choice books & 4 *Bulletins* (UK £65, Europe £85, ROW £120)
**World Poetry**
**8 Books:** 4 Choices, 4 Translation books & 4 *Bulletins* (£98, £160, £190)
**Complete**
**24 Books:** 4 Choices, 16 Recommendations, 4 Translations & 4 *Bulletins* (£230, £290, £360)
**Single copies of the *Bulletin*** £12.99

**Cover Artwork:** 'Bring Them In' by Moira Frith www.moirafrith.co.uk @moirafrith
With thanks to The Old School Gallery in Alnmouth www.theoldschoolgallery.co.uk

**Copyright** Poetry Book Society and contributors. All rights reserved.
ISBN 9781913129781   ISSN 0551-1690

Poetry Book Society | Milburn House | Dean Street | Newcastle upon Tyne | NE1 1LF
0191 230 8100 | enquiries@poetrybooksociety.co.uk

WWW.POETRYBOOKS.CO.UK

# LETTER FROM THE PBS

We have some wonderfully strong selections for you this Summer, with Fiona Benson and *Midden Witch* our Choice for the season. Across the recommendations expect powerful and empowering poetry addressing historical wrongs, personal trauma and disability while celebrating the power of nature and the natural world. It's wonderful to have an anthology in the recommendations; *Versus Versus* is an important new anthology, edited by Rachael Boast, including an international selection of deaf, disabled and neurodivergent poets. A really inspiring read.

Our podcast with Fiona Benson in partnership with Arji's Poetry Pickle Jar is now live. We hope this helps give some extra audio context to our brilliant Choice poet and her new collection. You can listen on our website or scan the QR code below.

Thank you so much to those of you who completed the online and paper surveys circulated to members recently. We particularly value your feedback, both positive and constructive, and will use the responses to inform our future plans. More on those in due course!

We have removed the full title listings from the *Bulletin* but wanted to assure readers that these titles are all included on our website (www.poetrybooks.co.uk) in one place, please click on the "Bookshop" tab, then "2025 Listings" and finally choose which period you are interested in i.e. "Summer 2025". If this does not suit you, please give us a phone call or email and we will happily send over the full list.

You'll see in this quarter's *Bulletin* we have included short bios on our guest reviewers – these are writers from the Ledbury Critics programme, The Writing Squad and Newcastle University's Creative Writing MA. Many of these writers are published poets themselves, so if you enjoyed their reviews please seek out their own poetry on our website too.

SOPHIE O'NEILL
PBS & INPRESS DIRECTOR

# MEET OUR SELECTORS

## BOOKS

Victoria Kennefick lives in Kerry. Her debut *Eat or We Both Starve* (Carcanet Press) won the Seamus Heaney First Collection Poetry Prize and was shortlisted for the T.S. Eliot Prize, the Costa Poetry Book Award, Derek Walcott Prize for Poetry, and the Butler Literary Prize. Her second book *Egg/Shell* was a PBS Spring Choice and she was an Arts Council of Ireland Writer-in-Residence.

Yomi Ṣode is a Nigerian British writer. His debut *Manorism* (Penguin) was shortlisted for the Rathbones Folio Prize, the T.S. Eliot Prize, the Brunel International and the African Poetry Prize. His one-man show *COAT* toured nationally and his play, *and breathe...* premiered at the Almeida Theatre. Yomi is founder of BoxedIN, First Five, The Daddy Diaries and 12 in 12.

## TRANSLATION

Shivanee Ramlochan is a Trinidadian writer. Her debut *Everyone Knows I Am a Haunting* (Peepal Tree Press) was shortlisted for the Forward Prize. Her poems are anthologised in *100 Queer Poems* (Faber); *After Sylvia* (Nine Arches Press) and *Across Borders: New Poetry from the Commonwealth* (Verve Poetry Press).

## PAMPHLETS

Yousif M. Qasmiyeh is a poet and translator with a doctorate from the University of Oxford. He was born and educated in Baddawi refugee camp in Lebanon. His debut *Writing the Camp* (Broken Sleep Books) was a PBS Recommendation and shortlisted for the Ondaatje Prize, followed by *Eating the Archive* (Broken Sleep Books).

Alycia Pirmohamed is the author of the PBS Recommendation *Another Way to Split Water*, Pamphlet Choice *Hinge* and a Nan Shepherd prize winning non-fiction book *A Beautiful and Vital Place*. She teaches at the University of Cambridge and co-founded the Scottish BPOC Writers Network.

# MEET OUR REVIEWERS

NASIM REBECCA ASL is an award-winning Glasgow-based poet. Her debut pamphlet *Nemidoonam* was released by Verve Poetry Press in 2023. Nasim was shortlisted for the 2025 Forward Poetry Prize for Best Single Poem – Performed.

DAVE COATES is a critic and essayist based in Edinburgh. He was a co-organiser of the Ledbury Critics Programme and is published in *Poetry Review, Poetry London, The Stinging Fly, Extra Teeth, catflap, spamzine*. He has reviewed for the *Bulletin* since 2021.

JENNY DANES is a poet and facilitator whose work has appeared in *Poetry Wales, The Rialto, Magma, Under the Radar, Basket,* and *bath magg*. In 2016 she won The Poetry Business' New Poets Prize, and her pamphlet *Gaps* was published by Smith|Doorstop. Find out more at www.jennydanes.co.uk.

BETH DAVIES is the current Sheffield Poet Laureate 2024-26. Her debut pamphlet *The Pretence of Understanding* was published by The Poetry Business in 2023 after winning the 2022 New Poets Prize. Find out more at bethdaviespoet.wordpress.com.

JASMINE GRAY is a Northern writer with art criticism and poetry published in *Anthropocene, The London Magazine,* and *The Double Negative*. She published two pamphlets with Broken Sleep Books, *Let's Photograph Girls Enjoying Life* (2019) and *Open Your Mouth* (2023).

KAYLEIGH JAYSHREE is a poet and reviewer. She is an alumna of the Roundhouse Collective and performed poetry at Glastonbury Festival. She has published reviews in *PN Review* and *Ink Sweat & Tears*. Her pamphlet is due out with fourteen poems.

GREGORY KEARNS is based in Liverpool. He was published in *Bath Magg, The Mersey Review* and *Not About Now* and has worked with English Heritage, No Dice Collective and Tmesis Theatre. He hosts The Poems We Made Along The Way podcast.

ROSE SCHIERIG is a poet and MA Writing Poetry student at Newcastle University. She graduated with a BA in English Literature with Creative Writing from Newcastle University in 2024. You can read her writing @fromrosamund on Instagram.

TAYIBA SULAIMAN is a writer and translator from Manchester. Her work has recently appeared in *Prospect Magazine, World of Interiors* and PEN *Transmissions*.

SHASH TREVETT is a poet and translator of Tamil poetry into English. Her collection *The Naming of Names* was published by Smith|Doorstop (2024). She is a Ledbury Critic and a Trustee of *Modern Poetry in Translation*.

# FIONA BENSON

Fiona Benson lives in Devon with her husband and their two daughters. She has published three previous collections of poetry, all of which were shortlisted for the T.S. Eliot Prize: *Bright Travellers*, which won the 2015 Geoffrey Faber Memorial Prize and the Seamus Heaney Centre for Poetry's Prize for First Full Collection; *Vertigo & Ghost*, which was shortlisted for the 2019 Rathbones Folio Prize and won both the Roehampton Poetry Prize and the Forward Prize for Best Collection; and *Ephemeron*, which was shortlisted for the Rathbones Folio Prize and the London Hellenic Prize.

# MIDDEN WITCH

CAPE POETRY | £13.00 | PBS PRICE £9.75

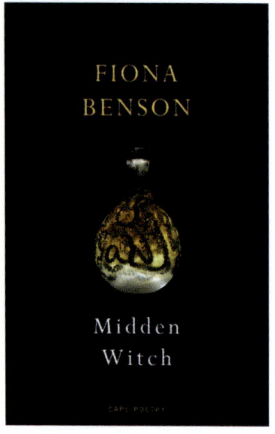

The provocative title of Fiona Benson's astonishing fourth collection *Midden Witch* suggests a figure who is a social pariah, tossed on the slag heap for outliving her usefulness, while simultaneously presenting as an unknowable danger in her guise as a misunderstood and reviled artist and healer. The collection is divided into six distinct but inevitably intertwined sections: 'Discovery of Witchcraft', 'Persecution', 'Herbals', 'Exorcisms', 'Familiars' and 'Folk Tales', which present as a definition, history, reclamation, explanation, botanical field guide and spellbook. This ingenious structure allows Benson to compile a comprehensive poetic compendium of witchcraft in all its iterations and manifestations.

> Once upon a witch

The first section 'Discovery of Witchcraft' begins with a short poem, more akin to an enchantment, anointing the eyes of the reader. Benson uses the incantatory language of archival accounts of witchcraft, dark humour and spell-like invocations to create a portal through which we gain access to tales of imagined transformations and instructions in hedge-magic. We meet Mary Hunter, Jenny Greenteeth and Leddy Lister and witness how these gifted, sometimes troubled, women became scapegoats, victims of societal paranoia and persecution, hounded for centuries, often to a gratuitously violent public execution.

The poems that form the 'Exorcism' section are as brilliant, shocking and utterly original a selection of poetry one can ever hope to experience where the legacy of healers, prodigies and sorceresses is passed through generations of women.

> Today I need an exorcism:
> there's a dead girl sleeping
> at the core of my house

Benson's poems traverse the boundaries of light and dark, weaving a shadow magic that holds both with equal weight and skill, before acknowledging that:

> The world is both crueller
> and lovelier than we know.

VICTORIA KENNEFICK

# FIONA BENSON

Midden Witch herself turned up first, hurt and spitting with fury. I tried to pursue her in further poems but she witched herself out of there pretty fast. I found some of her sisters in the archives at Palace Green Library in Durham and Exeter Cathedral Library, weary of misinterpretation, and then ransacked the old persecutory texts: preposterous allegations stacked up against women who did not have the means to defend themselves.

At the heart of all the witch furore there lies a deep fear of loss; a preoccupation with protecting loved ones against dark forces roaming through the world – call those forces witchcraft or infection, bedevilment or disease. Childhood illness, in particular, was so often fatal back then, and so difficult to understand. I feel keenly the irony of human beings engaging in ritual practices – i.e. witchcraft – to deflect the witch; as we still try (desperately, ineffectually) to protect the ones we love, even if it is only by making poems that are part spell, part prayer – to bind malice, to exorcise bad words, to ward off danger.

I also wanted to recoup some of our traditional folk tales, to claim again that mutable and magical world of stories told by women about women. And as a woman who brings home half-dead field mice or a broken rook, I was fascinated by the witch's familiar, which so dominated descriptions of witch-practices in the British Isles (on the Continent they were more exercised by the idea of the witches' ride; here we were fascinated by their pets).

The position of witches as scapegoats in their community is compelling in the modern-day context of contempt for middle-aged and older women, felt especially sharply as I stumble and trip my way through perimenopause, disappearing and dismissed. I consider my own tenuous position alongside normal society, wandering the Devon hedgerows and ditches, not a stay-at-home Mum, not a properly employed human, mumbling bits of poems, fretting about the sudden ramshackle disintegration of my body, the impossible hairs on my chin – what am I, if not a witch?

## FIONA RECOMMENDS

Artur Dron's *We Were Here* (Jantar Publishing) translated from the Ukrainian by Yuliya Musakovska; soldier-poet Artur Dron's poems are clear-sighted agonising accounts of trench warfare in Ukrainia. Dron was only twenty-two when he wrote these extraordinary pieces. Marie Howe, *What the Earth Seemed To Say: New & Selected* (Bloodaxe Books); Tracy K. Smith, *Such Color: New & Selected Poems* (Graywolf Press). And I am a bit obsessed with Ada Limón right now: *The Hurting Kind*, *The Carrying* and *Bright Dead Things* (all Corsair).

# RITE

Today I need an exorcism:
there's a dead girl sleeping
at the core of my house,
there are black crows falling
from the roof of my mouth –

I want to walk raw and clean into morning
    *the most high God commands you*
barefoot in the garden,
sun-warmed and nettle-stung,
    *God's word made flesh commands you*

a sprig of rowan in my hand
a hawthorn-leaf on my tongue,
    *the power of the Mysteries commands you –*
not this taste of tar and ash,
this dust-sheet shroud.

Evict the bitch, no matter
how she writhes and spits,
cast all my demons out.

# BLUEBELLS

Be wary in the woods; the wet blue pools
of bluebells hung with spells
are a well-managed enchantment.
Such doctoring is danger to a human child.
So do not let your children wander,
like that boy left to wade ungoverned,
who was locked in deep pockets of oak and song,
fed green broth of garlic and hawthorn,
and glamoured so none could find him,
though we called through the hours to bring him home.
The year turned bitter before he returned,
crept up to his mother's hearth – half-starved,
shivering and dazed – fairy-strayed,
tuned to the habits of the woods and strange,
running in his sleep with the deer.
On the longest night we went with lamps
to the darkest part of the woods and left him there.

Image: Jolade Olusanya

# ISABELLE BAAFI

Isabelle Baafi is a poet, editor and critic. Her pamphlet *Ripe* (ignitionpress) won the Somerset Maugham Award and was a Poetry Book Society Pamphlet Choice. Her poetry and prose have been published in the *TLS*, the *Poetry Review*, the *London Magazine*, *Oxford Poetry* and more.

# CHAOTIC GOOD

FABER & FABER    |    £ 12.99    |    PBS PRICE £9.75

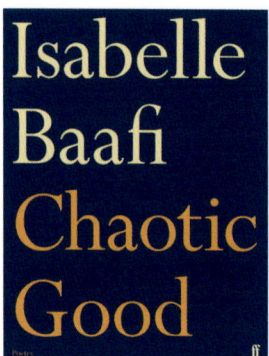

Charting the dissolution of a marriage with considerable ingenuity and skill, Baafi's debut pushes against the expectations we have of ourselves and our relationships, and how the disintegration of these, in times of crisis, can make freedom and self-actualisation a possibility. Each of the five sections of the book explores a different stage of personal development: SEPARATION, CHILDHOOD, ADOLESCENCE, MARRIAGE and REBIRTH with poems that echo the constant tension between rupture and repair, as we move through these states.

In 'Everything is going according to plane' Baafi rewrites her formative years employing deliberate mondegreens to do so, "In my pregnant mother's rind, I was perfect: my skin / as soft as a cotton bull". The effect is mesmerising, allowing the reader to simultaneously read two poems, experiencing a profound cognitive dissonance throughout, as though there exists a shadow poem of expectation lurking beneath the jarring truth in the speaker's language.

> Screaming
> to resist the void. Singeing in the dark.

The MARRIAGE section opens with 'Horizon Effect', "O first love, / blessed and cursed love, shelter me" which brilliantly plays with the computer gaming concept whereby the number of possible outcomes that a program can predict is limited, meaning the program may make a detrimental move because it cannot see its error. Baafi's poems grapple with interrogating balance and the inevitable losses and gains experienced in our search for it.

> Wondering if the light we destroy
> is brighter than the light still to come.

The concept of chaotic good represents a willingness to challenge authority and break rules to achieve positive change, and Baafi encourages us to re-examine what we consider to be mistakes or missteps. The collection itself is an act of reclamation through self-discovery and serves as a reminder that at the end of a cycle of hard times, we are 'Still Here'.

> Dividing lies by the truth I made,
> charting my future
> by the prophecy I became.

VICTORIA KENNEFICK

# ISABELLE BAAFI

From a phenomenological standpoint, time, by its very nature, is always coming or going but never here. The result is that it always seems to be slipping away from us, unravelling in our hands like an old (pun intended) piece of cloth on which is woven the story of our lives. And although free will is inalienable, and inextricably intertwined with one's morality, we live in a world with social structures and belief systems that engender inequality and deny agency to certain people more than others – women and girls especially.

All of this may converge to produce a sense of powerlessness, guilt, regret. In such a state, contending with the choices we've made – the effects we've caused, the selves we've become – proves difficult. Thoughts about who we are branch off like languages, accruing more and more disparate meanings that are both equally true but, eventually, so distantly related that it's hard for one part of us to converse with the other. The sense of duplicity is inherent; the feeling of betrayal is excruciating. When one's agency is constrained and the future seems unbearable, the urge to go back and rewrite the past is irresistible. But how can it be done?

Lyric poetry – a genre that often presents the self in a state of suspended time, fragmented physicality, and syntactical rebellion – lends itself to the quest of return and reclamation. Working with forms that invoke repetition, and inventing others that dramatise error and regret, rupture and repair, cyclicality and propulsion, became central to my poetic practice.

I reckon I understand Gatsby more than most people, improbable as he may seem. I think Zora Neale Hurston's protagonist Janie is one of literature's most overlooked feminist icons. And when Kierkegaard wrote that, "Life can only be understood backwards; but it must be lived forwards", I suspect he was remembering what would one day happen to me. Until time travel is discovered, we can't go back and rewrite the past. But opportunities for the (re)discovery of our power and agency through poetry may be the next best thing.

## ISABELLE RECOMMENDS

Raymond Antrobus, *Signs, Music* (Picador); Khairani Barokka, *amuk* (Nine Arches Press); Fiona Benson, *Vertigo & Ghost* (Cape); Jericho Brown, *The New Testament* (Picador); Anne Carson, *The Beauty of the Husband* (Cape); Imtiaz Dharker, *The Shadow Reader* (Bloodaxe); Vievee Francis, *The Shared World* (Northwestern University Press); Ella Frears, *Goodlord* (Rough Trade); Hasib Hourani, *rock flight* (Prototype); Rachel Mann, *Eleanor Among the Saints* (Carcanet); Carl Phillips, *Scattered Snows, to the North* (Carcanet Press); Charlotte Shevchenko Knight, *Food for the Dead* (Cape).

# EXIT INTERVIEW

I've started ending phone calls like on TV –
quick and heartless. The goodbye is implied.
A *need* becomes a *needle* if we let it.

My mother always said,
*If you reach a fork in the road, go right.*
But what if the right path is not the right path?

The way out is steeper than the way in.
But when a road reveals itself out of nowhere, I take it.
I take the coarse road and I don't look back.

In truth, I leave the way my father left:
piece by piece. My favourite books
and sharpest cutlery in the room across town

that I told myself I had rented 'for my writing';
my wedding ring gathering dust on a shelf
next to the watch I kept trying to give away.

And the apps I hid from view, the friends
I never introduced him to. The dream in which I shut
a corridor of doors, one by one. Peace by peace.

I choose right. I choose what's right.
I choose left. I choose what's left. I am the one
who soils my sheets and the one who cleans them.

# THE COTTAGE

The memory built me around it.
An abandoned trail. A forest with no sky.
I was both the wood of the axe

and the wood of the tree.
A cat was dying in my bag,
and when the leaves looked away

I snuck it crushed berries from the path
and dead sparrows whose hearts
had burst out of their chests.

The scarlet stained my palm –
whether the blood of the berry or of the bird,
I couldn't tell.

I was thirsty but afraid to drink.
When I reached the cottage,
you were waiting. You led me inside.

I offered you my hand, which you licked.
It was cleaner then
than it had ever been before.

Then you placed my hand on the door,
told me to cure it.
The door disappeared beneath my hand.

Image: Rebecca MacPhail

# ED. RACHAEL BOAST

Rachael Boast is a writer and editor. Her debut collection, *Sidereal* (Picador, 2011), won the Forward Prize for Best First Collection and the Seamus Heaney Centre First Collection Poetry Prize, and was followed by *Pilgrim's Flower* (Picador, 2013), shortlisted for the Griffin Poetry Prize. *Void Studies* (Picador, 2016) was shortlisted for the T.S. Eliot Prize. Her most recent collection is *Hotel Raphael* (Picador, 2021). Rachael co-edited *The Echoing Gallery: Bristol Poets and Art in the City* (Redcliffe Press, 2013) and *The Caught Habits of Language: An Entertainment for W.S. Graham for Him Having Reached One Hundred* (Donut Press, 2018). She is a Fellow of the Royal Society of Literature.

**Image Description:** A side-on photograph in close-up of a woman with short brown hair, wearing a grey fedora hat with a black band, grey scarf and jumper. She is standing in a wide stairwell in Glasgow's Mitchell Library, pillars in the background, is smiling and looking straight ahead.

# VERSUS VERSUS

BLOODAXE BOOKS | £14.99 | PBS PRICE £11.25

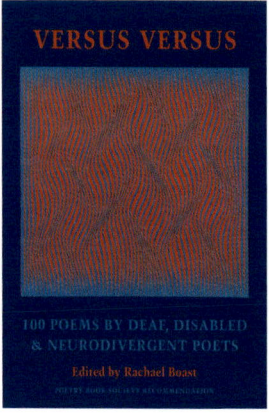

Edited by Rachael Boast, *Versus Versus* is a powerful anthology that brings together one hundred deaf, disabled and neurodivergent poets in a testament to resilience, community, and the power of lived experience. From the opening pages, the book pulses with urgency and solidarity.

These poets share their truths unapologetically, challenging perceptions, while celebrating togetherness. Leah Lakshmi Piepzna-Samarasinha's 'Crip fairy godmother' encapsulates the book's spirit:

> Disability is adaptive, interconnected, tenacious, voracious, slutty, silent,
>     raging,
> life giving
>
> We are crip Earthseed
> but we are not going anywhere
> You are not an individual health defect
> You are a systemic war battalion
> You come from somewhere
> You are a we

Some poems confront and disrupt, forcing the reader to sit with discomfort, while others feel like moments of stillness – holding time in their hands, as in Masaoka Shiki's poem '1898 Summer', translated by John Newton Webb.

> Put the chair there –
> where my knees
> will touch the roses

The title *Versus Versus* suggests a paradox: instead of pitching one against the other, there's strength in numbers as these nationally and internationally acclaimed poets unite to redress lingering misconceptions. Boast's introduction provides valuable context, emphasising that these contributors are not just poets but also novelists, essayists, children's authors and more, highlighting the depth of their creative contributions. *Versus Versus* is an essential read. It is loving and deeply moving. If you enjoy poetic forms then be prepared to swoon at the mix of sonnets, haikus, rengas, sign language, prose poems and much more. Reflecting diverse voices and experiences, this anthology is a gift – one that demands your time.

**I SELECTOR'S COMMENT**

YOMI ṢODE

# RACHAEL BOAST

In recent years there's been a sustained effort within the UK publishing industry to address the historical under-representation of authors from minority backgrounds. With a broader, enriched landscape now emerging, disability may be thought of as a forgotten diversity. This "forgetting" is part of an historically entrenched position – it's easier to forget than to provide for – and when deaf, disabled or neurodivergent people are reduced to the status of economic burden or stigmatised person in societies around the world this seeps into other aspects of life and it becomes easier to normalise lack of provision and discriminatory practices.

Anthologies are about bringing people together, creating community and, as in the case of *Versus Versus*, can be a radical act of resistance, education and joy. *Versus Versus* is also an anthology that, like its predecessors, continues the push for inclusion and explores in depth the subject of its lack across social, cultural, clinical and political settings worldwide.

The scope of the book's internationality is particularly important, allowing for a comprehensive range of subject matter and style. The contents are wide-ranging yet, at the same time, offer a poem-road that weaves between theme and context, pitch and texture.

It's rare for an anthology to be given a Recommendation by the Poetry Book Society so I would like to thank the selectors for recognising the book's vitality and the quality of the work it contains. Jean-Michel Basquiat knew how to upend cultural and societal impasse through his art, and his work inspired the anthology's title. The front cover features *Concurrent Colors*, a painting by the Polish artist and Siberian Gulag survivor, Julian Stanczak. *Versus Versus* is supported by the Royal Society of Literature through their Literature Matters Award and was prepared with the help of an Advocacy and Advisory Panel: Chisom Okafor, Karthika Naïr and Daniel Sluman.

## RACHAEL RECOMMENDS

Eds. Sandra Alland, Khairani Barokka and Daniel Sluman, *Stairs and Whispers: D/deaf and Disabled Poets Write Back* (Nine Arches Press); Eds. Lisa Kelly and Sophie Stone, *What Meets the Eye? The Deaf Perspective* (Arachne Press); Eds. Mohammad Awad, Radhiah Chowdhury and David Stavanger, *Admissions: Voices within Mental Health* (Upswell Poetry); Eds. Andy Jackson, Esther Ottaway and Kerri Shying, *Raging Grace: Australian Writers Speak Out on Disability* (Puncher & Wattmann).

# ESSAY FRAGMENT:
## MEDICAL MODEL OF DISABILITY

The ~~disabled~~ body is always closest　　　to machine
in its dysfunction.　　　Most fixable
when it is furthest from human　　　body
as metaphor/rhetorical question:
If a clock is broken　　　do you repair it　　　or
ask the world to conform　　　to its sense of time.[1]
~~Disabled~~ body as abnormality.　　　Outlier
that must be removed　　　from the data
for more *accurate* results.　　　Medical Model [2]　speaks
says people [with disabilities] need to work　　　harder
to overcome [themselves].　　　The cure is to make them
*more normal.*[3]　　my ~~disabled~~ body is a price tag
is scalpel bait　　　a prayer to hospital ceilings
or my ~~disabled~~ body is a weight on society.[4]
The Medical Model says:　　　my ~~disabled~~ body
is like any disease.　　　If we discover a new & hungry
sickness　　　is it our duty to cure it　　or to let it be?

---

1 You must fix what is holding you back.
2 Formally *Functional-Limitation Model*; formally *Biological-Inferiority Model*.
3 Read: less disabled.
4 Another price tag.

From *Wound from the Mouth of a Wound* © 2020 by torrin a. greathouse. Reprinted with permission of The Permissions Company LLC on behalf of Milkweed Editions.

**Image Description:** The book's cover features a square-shaped artwork entitled *Concurrent Colors* (1965) by Polish artist, Julian Stanczak © Julian Stanczak Foundation. The painting creates an optical illusion of vertical moving curved lines in red and blue, giving the impression of moving waves or sand dunes. At the edges of the painting the lines thin out so that they resemble a comb effect.

Image: Adela Fernandez

# MOYA CANNON

Moya Cannon is an Irish poet with six previous collections. She was brought up in an Irish speaking family in Co. Donegal, received a BA in History and Politics from University College, Dublin, and an MPhil in International Relations from Corpus Christi College, Cambridge. A recipient of the inaugural Brendan Behan Award and the O'Shaughnessy Award, she was Heimbold Professor of Irish Studies at Villanova University and in 2004 was elected to Aosdána, the affiliation of Irish creative artists. Her work has been widely anthologised and translated and she has read at festivals and universities in Europe, Asia and the Americas.

# BUNTING'S HONEY

CARCANET PRESS | £ 11.99 | PBS PRICE £9.00

Moya Cannon's seventh book of poetry opens with an epigraph from Rainer Maria Rilke which includes the lines, "We are the bees of the invisible. We wildly collect the honey of the visible, to store it in the great golden hive of the invisible." The book's title is taken from a poem central to its themes of music, nature, history and the role of the artist, which was commissioned by Cruit Éireann (Harp Ireland) and set to music by harpist, Aisling Lyons, to mark the 250th anniversary of the birth of Edward Bunting (1773–1843). Bunting – a music collector, publisher, editor and organist – is credited with saving the music of the Irish harp for posterity, at a time when it was in danger of permanent loss.

Rilke's declaration and Bunting's radical action are, for Cannon, a blueprint for the function of the artist as an observer, collector, curator and a channel for the natural creative impulse that is one and the same as the honeybee's drive to make and to store honey.

> for what do a musician's hands ever hold
> but the hammered treasure of the human soul?

From Blaise Pascal in the poem 'Pascal':

> (who) understood so much as (he) stood in awe
> of our long-armed swirl of stars
> burning their huge hearts out

to 'Monet in Árann' and "the blurry summery sway of it", Cannon draws parallels between our immediate experiences of nature while also acknowledging how it is unavoidably coloured by artists' rendering of it. This is not an interruption or distraction in the poems, rather it is an addition to "the great golden hive of the invisible." The musicality of Cannon's work is harmonious and intoxicating throughout, with resonances of her background in traditional Irish music that echo her fluency in the Irish language. The seemingly effortless symphony of these elements combines in Cannon's work, so it sings off the page.

> the sea, the sea
> sky-mirror, mood-mirror, old friend.

VICTORIA KENNEFICK

I SELECTOR'S COMMENT

# MOYA CANNON

Sometimes I feel like a turnstone, the quick little bird that tosses over pebbles on the beach in search of the nourishment lying beneath. Nobody knows where a poem might be found, or, more likely, where a poem might find its writer. It is hard to say why particular moments of our lives are illuminated or why incidents or experiences can lodge in the heart, mind and body, sometimes for years, asking to be voiced.

As with my previous collections, our physical, emotional, aesthetic and spiritual links to sea, shore and mountains are a central theme in this book, as is the layering of human histories, from the personal to the political, which mark and make a place. Increasingly, though, a lower note resonates as "the peace of wild things" (Wendell Berry) and wild places come so seriously under threat from our human recklessness.

Music, like visual art, is one of the channels which gives us a sense of the inner lives of our human predecessors, their griefs, gaieties and passions. The title poem, 'Bunting's Honey', relates to the Belfast Harp festival of 1792, when nineteen-year-old Edward Bunting was commissioned to collect the music of the surviving itinerant Irish harpers, awakening his life-long interest in the ancient harp airs and the harpers who were the custodians of that music.

Many of the poems are grounded in Ireland whereas others have been sparked by encounters with other grounds and cultures. There are a number of elegies and since, unfortunately, we live again in deeply troubled times, war has made its way into the poems too. In the final section, a clutch of poems returns to the territory of much of my first collection, the magical, resonant karst landscape of The Burren in County Clare.

## MOYA RECOMMENDS

I meander between recent publications and old favourites. Some of the collections which I found most moving over the past few years were Eva Bourke, *Tattoo* (Dedalus Press); Kerry Hardie, *We Go On* (Bloodaxe); Paula Meehan, *The Solace of Artemis* (Dedalus Press) and Eiléan Ní Chuilleanáin, *The Map of the World* (Gallery Press). Two very striking and skilled collections by younger writers are Seán Hewitt's *Tongues of Fire* (Cape) and Oksana Maksymchuk's *Still City* (Carcanet). In these terrible times of war I return to Naomi Shihab Nye's *Tender Spot* (Bloodaxe). With undimmed admiration I have been rereading Louis MacNeice, Tomas Tranströmer, Jane Hirshfield and Mary Oliver.

in the blurry, summery sway of it

Image: *The Pink Bush* by Joseph Quilty

# THIS MORNING

*for Jean Tuomey*

This morning by the sun-bashed sea,
in which I have swum for ten minutes,
I feel younger than when I was young
in spite of my sixty-six circuits of the sun.

I have done nothing to earn joy
or health, yet today, am flooded with both.
I want to bottle this morning in a song
so that, some hail-smitten, hope-poor

winter's day, it can be poured out—
sun on salted pebbles and on me,
a flutter-swoop of sand-martins
and the whispers of a June sea.

Image: Derrick Kakembo

# PASCALE PETIT

Pascale Petit was born in Paris, grew up in France and Wales, and now lives in Cornwall. She is of French, Welsh, and Indian heritage. Her seventh collection *Mama Amazonica* (2017), a Poetry Book Society Choice, won the RSL Ondaatje Prize and The Laurel Prize. Her eighth, *Tiger Girl* (2020), was shortlisted for the Forward Prize for Best Collection and for the English language poetry category of Wales Book of the Year 2021. Four of her earlier six collections were shortlisted for the T.S. Eliot Prize, while a portfolio from *Fauverie* won the Manchester Poetry Prize. Her ninth collection *Beast* (2025) is her third publication with Bloodaxe Books.

# BEAST

BLOODAXE BOOKS | £12.99 | PBS PRICE £9.75

Poet, mentor and friend, Tshaka Campbell once told me to "listen different". Whether I am watching a performance or reading a poem, he would say the same thing, over and over, "listen different". His request (while it seemed simple) required me to tune into a new frequency. I read Pascale Petit's ever-growing contribution to poetry and I'm reminded of this saying. Her latest offering *Beast* resumes Petit's universe of nature and wilderness. Those who have ventured through her past works will be familiar with the landscape. To some degree you know the layout, the smells and feels and yet, with *Beast*, it's as though you have uncovered an additional layer.

> The moment I was born, you were a screw worm
> feeding on my navel.
>
> While I was a baby, you became a botfly
> which bored through my fontanelle, lodged in my brain.
>
> So when I learnt to talk, I named you:
> Yellow Jack, Blue Devil, Black Vomit.
>
> I watched you fly away from my childhood
> to eat the face of God.

I think of my own career, questioning longevity and where new concepts will sprout from. In *Beast*, you are submerged in mythic and warped realities. An encyclopedia of animals, insects and endangered species weaved into a tale of survival, family and our current climate. Petit's exploration of childhood makes you question the many things we navigate to get us through the most difficult times. It is the face we show as though everything were ok, the imaginary friend when no one listens, or the closest people resurfacing as objects or animals.

As though this collection is a type of frequency to tune into, let it open the channel of imagination in all of us, when dealing with the most delicate matters, step by step. Petit's universe continues to grow, and I am thankful.

YOMI ṢODE

# PASCALE PETIT

My approach to extinction is personal, linked to my childhood, and how animals healed me and helped me love my abusive parents. As Earth descends into climate catastrophe and is beset by wildfires, territorial conflicts, and plagues, *Beast* suggests there is a connection between planetary abuse and the abuse of women and children in the family. It is also a quest to record the ferocity and ineffable beauty of wild animals as they become increasingly endangered. Each of the five sections focuses on a different wilderness or place of conflict, and its wildlife.

It opens with Amazonia, the last refuge of a pristine habitat, where I am able to love my mentally ill mother by transforming her into a rainforest. She morphs into a catfish, jaguar, shoal of piranhas and a piano. My father appears as a trophy hunter and as a botfly. He once lived in Provence, so the next part of the book is set in the south of France, where he is evoked in the Camargue, its wild bulls and horses, as well as the mythical monsters that haunt the fertile Rhône delta, such as the hybrid Tarasque and pan-like Beast of Vaccarès. I spent two summers in these lush marshes, observing nests of white storks and heronries among woods echoing with nightingale song, researching its myths and discovering its extraordinary fauna. The nearby Languedoc is filled with memories of my mother in an overgrown vineyard when I was a child. It also has dark legends, such as the Bête du Gévaudan, a man-eating wolf, while the limestone plateaux called "causses", are a temporary home to the almost extinct Takhi horses.

At the heart of this collection is a long prose poem 'Tala Zone' which takes place simultaneously in a Paris cellar and in Bandhavgarh's tiger forests, where vestiges of the animal kingdom are protected. I lived in Paris with my father as a child, and it is in the cellar of our apartment block that I encounter his ghost, and where wonders of my Indian grandmother's homeland come to my rescue. After these subterranean terrors, the following section is a short personal response to the genocide in Gaza. *Beast* ends on my local Bodmin Moor, where I walked every day during lockdown, accompanied by its own beast.

## PASCALE RECOMMENDS

Mosab Abu Toha, *Forest of Noise* (4th Estate); Sarah Holland-Batt, *The Jaguar* (Bloodaxe Books); Romalyn Ante, *AGIMAT* (Chatto); Karen Downs-Barton, *Minx* (Chatto); Jorie Graham, *To 2040* (Carcanet); Niall Campbell, *The Island in the Sound* (Bloodaxe Books); Tishani Doshi, *A God at the Door* (Bloodaxe Books); Mei-mei Berssenbrugge, *Hello, the Roses* (New Directions); Warsan Shire, *Bless the Daughter Raised by a Voice in Her Head* (Chatto); Ruth Padel, *Girl* (Chatto); Alice Hiller, *bird of winter* (Pavilion Poetry); Yvonne Reddick, *Burning Season* (Bloodaxe Books); Dzifa Benson, *Monster* (Bloodaxe Books).

I clung to his back and rode my life

Image: *Sans titre* by Eugenio Santoro (2020) from the Collection de l'Art Brut, Lausanne (Suisse)

# A MOTHER SINGS

I have tucked my daughter back
into my womb.

I have taken her through my Red Sea.
Bomb blasts are muffled there.

She no longer has to breathe poisonous air.
She is cushioned from shrapnel.

She doesn't have to run on premature legs.
Her lungs are tamarisks where doves perch.

My breasts prepare her milk and honey.
They sing to her of paradise.

I will rebirth her on banks of the river of life.
I'll wade through the river of thorns

while she still sleeps.
I am her country and her lagoon.

I've draped my bones with hanging gardens
for her to crawl into when she arrives.

Image: Esther Cow

# CATHERINE-ESTHER COWIE

Catherine-Esther Cowie was born in St Lucia to a Tobagonian father and a St Lucian mother. She migrated with her family to Canada and then to the USA. Her poems have been published in *PN Review*, *Prairie Schooner*, *West Branch Journal*, *The Common*, *SWWIM*, *Rhino Poetry* and others. She is a Callaloo Creative Writing Workshop fellow.

# HEIRLOOM

CARCANET PRESS | £11.99 | PBS PRICE £9.00

Catherine-Esther Cowie's debut *Heirloom* is a breathtaking exploration of generational trauma, resilience, and the haunting persistence of history. In a canon reminiscent of literary greats like Toni Morrison and Zora Neale Hurston, Cowie crafts a narrative that spans four generations of women, each carrying the weight of their past while searching for light in the darkness. The strength of *Heirloom* lies in its portrayal. The recollections of these women are raw and harrowing, forcing readers to confront cycles of violence that feel eerily relevant to contemporary struggles. Yet, Cowie does not allow suffering to become the defining element of her characters. Beneath the pain, there is a quiet but undeniable resilience – one that seeps through each story, each memory, each attempt to break free.

How did she find the axe?

She wouldn't eat the fruit,
refused its sweetness,

weight of our father,
the first city.

Lord, she went down to the garden,
an axe flowering in her hand.

[...]

we were hungry, Lord.

The tree fell into the house.

What elevates this collection is Cowie's use of language. The colloquial elements and cultural traditions woven throughout add a spiritual depth, grounding the narrative in a sense of place and heritage. *Heirloom* examines the ways trauma can be inherited and resisted, yet Cowie reminds us that survival is not just about endurance; it is about transformation and pulling through when feeling the weight of it all. As with most poetry collections that I'm thankful to read, it made me question how best to navigate the current world I'm living in. A remarkable debut from Catherine-Esther Cowie that's worth reading and discussing afterwards.

SELECTOR'S COMMENT

YOMI ṢODE

# THE OUTSIDE CHILD

I will not disappear, dead myself
in a bush somewhere.
The freak lives, sucks air.
I have a face that is not so unlike hers.
Perhaps that's what troubles,
I am the final blow. The betrayal,
so close, under her roof, in her bed.
The man she so loved, loved me,
raised me in her house, unnatural thing that I am,
a sin, offspring of a predator and a prey,
that grows and grows, has a mammalian face,
hands, feet, a voice like the blackbird's,
high-pitched and singing.

In my wildest dreams, I hug her
children, my cousins.
They are my brothers and sisters.
How they insult, *mother-killer,*
*daughter of a sketel.*
I blossom bright, draw nearer still,
allow their biting, bites. The sharp of their teeth,
the only intimacy:
my flesh an epiphany.
                I am, love me.

Image: Luke Eastop

Image: Sarah Annie

# JESSICA TAGGART ROSE

# CLAIRE DURAND-GASSELIN

Jessica Taggart Rose is a writer and editor fascinated by human nature, the nature of time and our interactions with the natural world. Her poems have been published in *Letters to the Earth*, *Storm Chasers* and *New Contexts* anthologies, *Confluence Magazine*, *Full House* and *Three Drops from a Cauldron*. A founding member of Poets for the Planet, she lives in Margate where she helps to run the Margate Bookie lit fest and Margate Stanza.

Claire Durand-Gasselin is a bilingual poet and visual artist. She lived in the US from 2014-22, and now resides in Montreuil, France. She is the cofounder and artistic director of Mad Gleam Press, and now works as a literary translator, specialising in poetry. She's also an editor and active member of Paris Lit Up. Her publications include *A Shape Produced by a Curve* (Great Weather For Media), *Revue Miroir*, the podcast *Mange tes Mots* and the website Synapse International.

# THE RIVER HAS NO COLOUR

JESSICA TAGGART ROSE, TRANS. CLAIRE DURAND-GASSELIN

THE NEW MENARD PRESS | £10.99 | PBS PRICE £8.25

Even in the most inert of seasons, life still flows through us. This is a central proposition of Jessica Taggart Rose's *The River Has No Colour*, featuring Taggart Rose's English language poems, flanked by Claire Durand-Gasselin's French translations. If a steadfastness of gaze is one of the chief markers of moving eco-poetry, this debut contains it, while wending its way beyond it: these poems do not observe only; they implicate themselves in their environment. The Seine is Taggart Rose's muse, a living, teeming abundance of apparitions and armaments, a liquid cavalcade of human and animal, vegetable and mineral. Home to:

> Joan of Arc's ashes;
> Brahim Bouarram,
> drowned by the far right;
> up to 200 Algerians
> killed by Parisian police
> and poet Paul Celan,
> a holocaust survivor,
> who died by suicide.

The poet's listing cleaves a memorial space down the spine of the river itself. How do the poems, arranged into the four temperate seasons, maintain a hold on everything the Seine has seen? They possess, unsurprisingly, an innate fluidity in both their original English and Durand-Gasselin's translations – they flow and meander, gathering bright, chaotic significances as they move.

An ancient river cannot be prescribed by a single story. These poems gather as many as they can hold, presenting them to the reader's gaze with curiosity and entrancement, in registers of warmth and intimacy. Taggart Rose's poetic generosities extend themselves to numerous italicised inclusions of the voices of other writers, channelling Henry Miller, Djuna Barnes, and Hope Mirrlees, who calls the Seine "an old egotist" who "meanders imperturbably towards the sea". Taggart Rose harnesses and tenderly addresses that grand ego, never trying to trap or tame it, revealing the myriad ways a river works upon the hearts and souls of those around it, claiming bodies, artefacts, histories, hearts.

SELECTOR'S COMMENT

SHIVANEE RAMLOCHAN

# DRINK

I pour out the last of a bottle, red.
Mark off names of streets
already walked, intersections
where *bridges end the lyric.*

The poetic corpus stifles
like summer apartment heat.
Fly-like, I circle poet corpses
on empty streets, cafes closed.

*The river motes all ways at once in time*

It's a different wine I drink,
vines drenched in too-hot sun,
grapes withering, parched
while humans remain
in their stupor.

*Water hour, the rubble barge
bears us to evening*

Italics: The first two quotes are from Douglas Oliver, *Arrondissements* (Salt Publishing, 2003). The third quote is from *Poems of Paul Celan* (Persea Books, 2002).

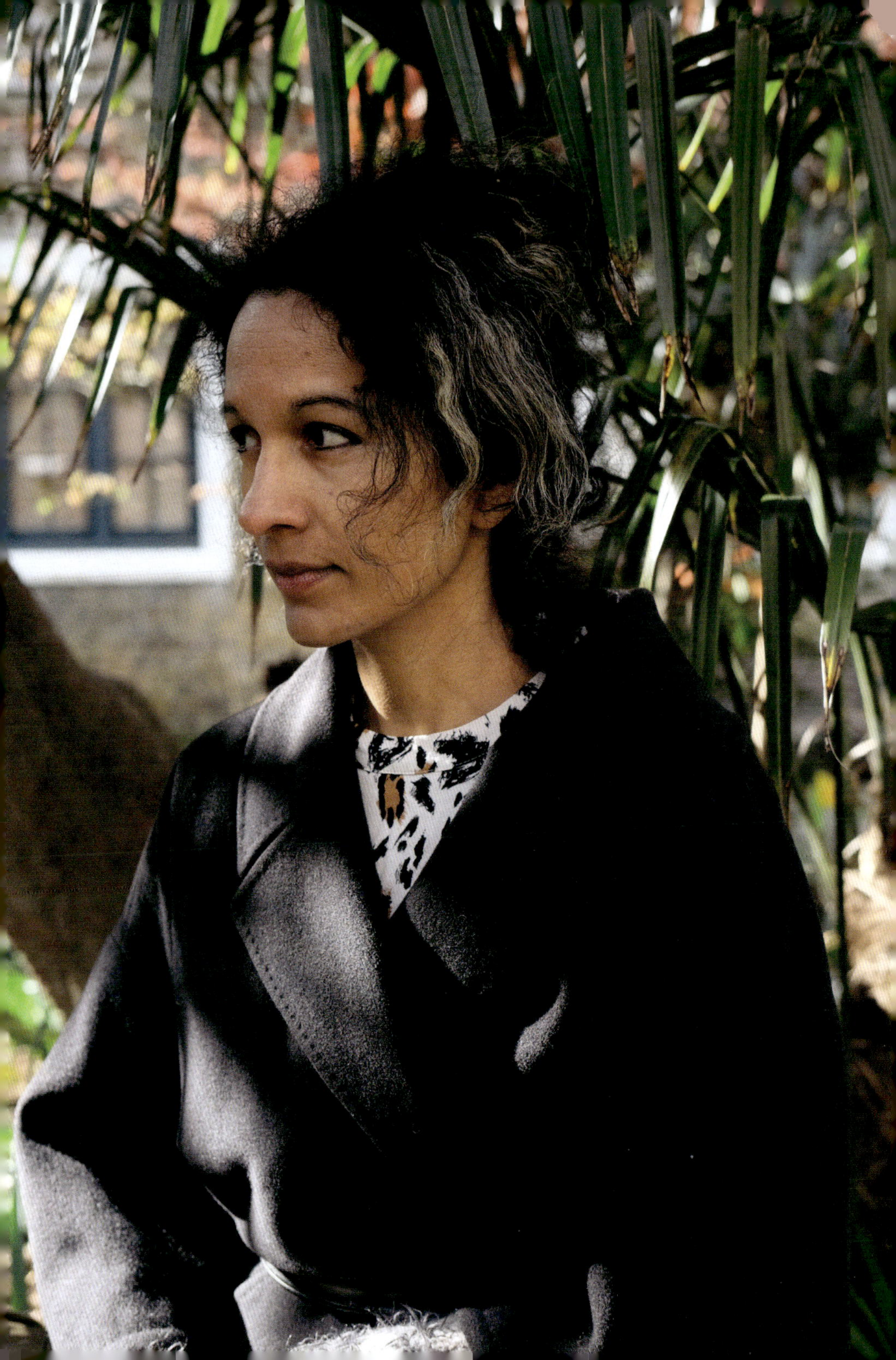

# RUSHIKA WICK

Rushika Wick's first poetry collection *Afterlife As Trash* (Verve, 2021) was highly commended in the Forward prizes and concerns selfhood and value in late stage capitalism. She runs sunseekers poetry project with Ana Seferović curating multidisciplinary and cross-modal events and an online archive and has collaborated with dancers, produced ekphrastic work for the National Gallery as well as visual poem objects and films. Her second book *Horse* (Broken Sleep, 2024) is a hybrid work on speculative archives.

# INFECTIONS OF LOSS
BROKEN SLEEP BOOKS  |  £7.99  |

The poems in *Infections of Loss* by Rushika Wick have the substance of dreams. Captivatingly ephemeral and imaginative, they "shimmer amphibian" and wander "temporal." Wick's speakers often straddle the jagged edges of time and memory, captioning the birds and blurs that move "in the corner of / the memory-mind" with innovative language and magnetic syntax; these lines ripple and contract, traversing the field of the page like a:

> great snake
> shedding spectres

In this collection, what is real and imagined coalesces, and images pair across endless spaces – including the generational, metaphysical, and national. This work is curious and inventive. It froths and hums and hungers. It shifts the recognisable into alluring and unfamiliar shapes.

> Rain spills from Gingko leaves
> divine choreography
> a mirror saying, *I am*,
> all the splinters in my flesh
> – my soles, palms,
> are asemic writing.
> I started to dance because
> I found it easier than talking,
> six responses to
> *do I smell nice?*
> I was a little case
> full of music cassettes,
> being played outside
> by the river.

In *Infections of Loss* Wick presses upon the natural world to capture the way "migration encircles / a petrified forest," and how inheritance makes one:

> an untouchable
> tideline with past lives.

These expressions of movement are especially evocative throughout, and, at times, undulate with an unsettling but breath-taking energy.

YOUSIF M. QASMIYEH & ALYCIA PIRMOHAMED

# GOOD LUCK TO YOU IN THE WORLD OF TEETH

Quiet in birth, astounded
swimming in smoke
before the police siren opera
kicks in (the door)
Your mother flounders in a
Mermaid Martini
each drink a sink
to keep her afloat.
See how she watches
the slight movement
of your chrysalis eyelids, filigree veins
flushed with life,
Moon Opal in a locket.
Truth is, that there's no room for
gentle souls like her.
The papers are readied but
how many people nearly die
trying their best to love?

# SUMMER BOOK REVIEWS

## MONA ARSHI & KAREN McCARTHY WOOLF: NATURE MATTERS
### REVIEWED BY NASIM REBECCA ASL

This gathering of over seventy-five poets of colour is nature writing at its most vivid. Across four elemental sections, these writers celebrate, observe and document the vastness of the earth in thunderous specificity, in poems that lap at the senses and eddy in the mind. From the "little snail" to the "edges of oceans", no corner is left unnoticed. *Nature Matters* is a paean to this planet and an urgent call to bear witness to the wonders of this world.

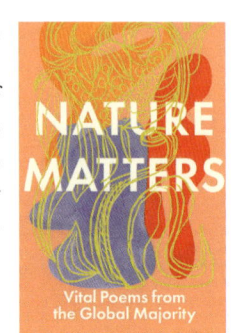

FABER & FABER | £14.99 | PBS PRICE £11.25

## LEO BOIX: SOUTHERNMOST: SONNETS
### REVIEWED BY SHASH TREVETT

An erudite collection, like a cabinet of curiosities, containing perfectly crafted sonnets intermingling history, mythology and natural historiography with meditations on homeland and family. The poems on colonial expansion into South America are superb: the poet equally a historian and a storyteller. There is a tenderness in this collection, with Boix coming full circle, reconciling the past (in loving poems to his mother) with the present (in love poems to his husband). A book which holds much weight and yields much satisfaction to the reader.

CHATTO & WINDUS | £12.99 | PBS PRICE £9.75

## BILLY COLLINS: WATER, WATER
### REVIEWED BY KAYLEIGH JAYSHREE

"He takes the deepest breath known to man, and, holding it, dives in," the speaker proclaims in Billy Collins' newest collection. Split into four parts, there's a pinch of irony, a fondness for enjambement and plenty of epiphanies to swim in. Find yourself in Philadelphia or Amsterdam, encounter death, fires, Emily Dickinson, and, of course, poetry itself. So take a deep breath (it doesn't have to be the deepest) and dive into sixty new poems that reignite, switch and surprise.

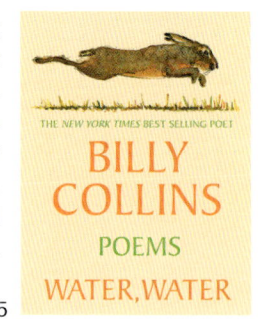

PICADOR | £12.99 | PBS PRICE £9.75

# WRITING SQUAD & LEDBURY CRITICS

## JEN HADFIELD: SELECTED POEMS
### REVIEWED BY GREGORY KEARNS

Hadfield's *Selected Poems* is filled with joyful invention: "bravery" becomes "tugsome", children's faces are illuminated by "omniscient / App-light", all of this paired with delicious wordplay like "chateau Neuf-de-Poop". Nothing escapes her attention between the "soil's dark meat" and the "shuddering stars". Hadfield's work is most effervescent when showing us what is off the beaten track; not just capturing how we imagine nature to be, but how it actually is, in all its strange messy g(l)ory.

PICADOR | £14.99 | PBS PRICE £11.25

## ERICA HESKETH: IN THE LILY ROOM
### REVIEWED BY JENNY DANES

This is a debut brimming with visceral, intricate poems on motherhood, mental health, and dreams. Hesketh is skilled at seamless tonal shifts; her poems often pivot neatly and without ceremony into the startling or surreal. The imagery is precise and vivid: a breast-feeding baby is a "hot-cheeked locksmith", menstrual blood clots are "fat slugs – beet, blackberry, rust". Other poems interrogate language itself: the word "mummy" is pulled apart and played with, while an abecedarian shows Hesketh's agility and craft.

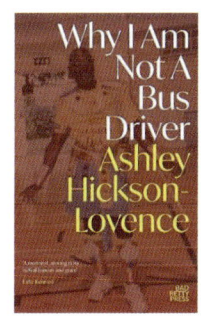

NINE ARCHES PRESS | £11.99 | PBS PRICE £9.00

## ASHLEY HICKSON-LOVENCE: WHY I AM NOT A BUS DRIVER
### REVIEWED BY JASMINE GRAY

Weaving elegy and the immediate in an irresistible rhythm, *Why I Am Not A Bus Driver* examines the ways a country, electric with life, can cling to the shadows of those we have lost. Movement is central to this collection, as we bop, drive and run away from conventional sonnets to a sometimes stark, more often thrillingly real, conversation. There is complex reflection and instruction from Hickson-Lovence here: we "don't need fancy poetry... just normal words... to slowly move on".

BAD BETTY PRESS | £10.99 | PBS PRICE £8.25

## SAFA KHATIB: A DRESS OF LOCUSTS
### REVIEWED BY DAVE COATES

Composed with bold, economical precision, Khatib's debut comprises a blend of dream, riddle, parable, and prophecy. The book's title is spoken by Ishtar, the Mesopotamian goddess of love and war. This is, incredibly, an apt punctum for the book's meditations on desire, faith, and ancient continuities between the so-called "West" and "(Middle) East". Khatib's wildly ambitious imagination collapses those divisions and defies contemporary geopolitical premises. The book's idiosyncratic spirituality and vision are matched by its delightful, playful earthiness. Essential reading.

BLOOMSBURY | £10.99 | PBS PRICE £8.25

## THEOPHILUS KWEK: COMMONWEALTH
### REVIEWED BY DAVE COATES

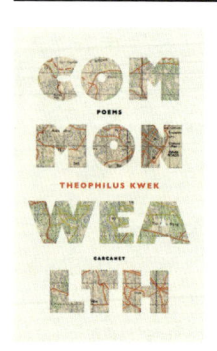

*Commonwealth* blossoms slowly, but satisfyingly. Its intimate, vivid, street-level journeys through personal and public archives portray the eponymous Singaporean neighbourhood over decades, its growths, losses, and endless reinvention. Kwek deftly weaves the historical threads of Singapore's colonial origins, with their fallout, on local people. By removing himself from the picture, he allows his (and the neighbourhood's) stories room to take root and grow, trusting the reader to handle them just as gracefully.

CARCANET PRESS | £12.99 | PBS PRICE £9.75

## ÉIREANN LORSUNG: PATTERN-BOOK
### REVIEWED BY ROSE SCHIERIG

*Pattern-book* is a meadow of poems, swaying between cycling seasons; a living hedgerow that teems with time-anchoring objects and flashes of the familiar, passer-by and out of reach. Sowed throughout *Pattern-book* are seeds collected from poets and artists, as Lorsung skilfully navigates time, grief, art and friendship. *Pattern-book* doubles-back and renews; snow melts into saplings, childhood becomes youth, becomes adulthood, and life begins, then ends, only to begin again.

CARCANET PRESS | £12.99 | PBS PRICE £9.75

## THERESA MUÑOZ: ARCHIVUM
### REVIEWED BY BETH DAVIES

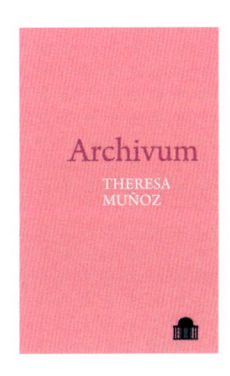

In *Archivum*, the past is both ever-present and always out of reach, as Muñoz's poems don white gloves to study "yellowed letters falling apart like crushed tulips". Fragments from the life of the author Muriel Spark overlap with thoughts of the speaker's lost loved ones, in tantalising attempts to reconstruct memory and history. Although a "letter isn't love", these poems pull the reader in, compelling us towards "holding / our past items up to the light. Hoping to see things through."

PAVILION POETRY | £10.99 | PSB PRICE £8.25

## VIDYAN RAVINTHIRAN: AVIDYĀ
### REVIEWED BY SHASH TREVETT

Through allegory, mythology and the examination of war, this is one of the best collections to explore being a Tamil from Sri Lanka. Navigating the conflict between "impulse and form" these poems seek to understand abandoned landscapes and history. Yet this is not a work of diasporan poetry: in *Avidyā*, Ravinthiran is as much a part of "there" as he is of "here". Finding peace within these pages, he speaks with authority as one who is embraced by a reclaimed heritage.

BLOODAXE BOOKS | £12.00 | PBS PRICE £9.00

## BENJAMIN ZEPHANIAH: DIS POETRY: SELECTED POEMS
### REVIEWED BY TAYIBA SULAIMAN

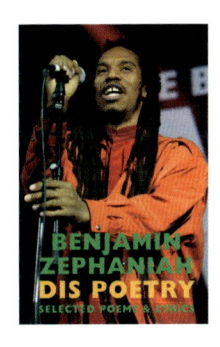

This collection honours Benjamin Zephaniah's lifelong commitment to speaking truth to power. The selected poems include everything from anarchist satires on our "green unpleasant land", to refugee retellings of Scottish folk tales, and verses raging against the racist murders of Black people and oppressed people everywhere. With links to live recordings embedded in the book, these poems of power and protest demand to be read aloud, so they can march off the page in search of justice.

BLOODAXE BOOKS | £12.99 | PBS PRICE £9.75

# PAMPHLET REVIEWS

## TOM BAILEY: PLEASE DO NOT TOUCH OR FEED THE HORSES
### REVIEWED BY ROSE SCHIERIG

*Please Do Not Touch or Feed the Horses* blends a thrumming web of life's connections with an overarching exploration of death's echoes. With playful wit punctuated by a cutting candour, Bailey injects the human into the natural world and the natural into the human world. These poems underline the vibrancy of the ordinary, picking out pearls of the day-to-day. Skilfully weaving states, *Please Do Not Touch or Feed the Horses* is a striking reminder of the multiplicity of life.

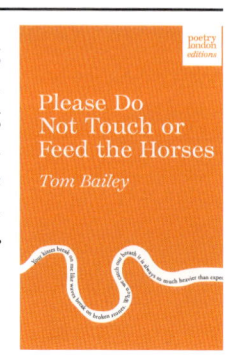

POETRY LONDON EDITIONS £5.00

## EVE ELLIS: SPIT VALVE
### REVIEWED BY ROSE SCHIERIG

*Spit Valve* navigates unearthly borderlands. These poems unfold at intersections of life and death, silence and noise, secrecy and truth. In these in-between spaces, Ellis digs into the skin of night and ice to address ancestral histories, where women's bodies are portrayed as ill, impacted and lost. In uncanny snapshots, *Spit Valve* considers how the past permeates the present. It wonders at the consequences of recognising and ignoring the persisting echoes of what came before.

IGNITION PRESS £7.00

## JEN FEROZE: A DRESS WITH DEEP POCKETS
### REVIEWED BY ROSE SCHIERIG

*A Dress with Deep Pockets* is a tender exploration of womanhood, motherhood and friendships that unfold in vivid fragments. In portraits of people and places, Feroze balances domestic worlds with natural spheres to create attentive and particular poems. Her poetry deals with memories of all kinds, the quiet and sonorous material of life. Navigating love, loss and longing, *A Dress with Deep Pockets* captures moments in time and holds them up to the light.

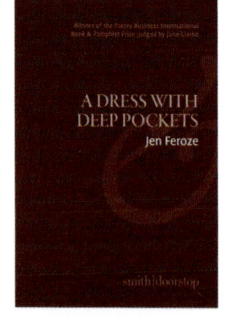

SMITH | DOORSTOP £6.00